AN AGE OF EXTREMES
1880-1917

STUDENT STUDY GUIDE

OXFORD

UNIVERSITY PRESS

OXFORD
UNIVERSITY PRESS

Oxford University Press, Inc., publishes works that
further Oxford University's objective of excellence
in research, scholarship, and education.

Oxford   New York
Auckland   Cape Town   Dar es Salaam   Hong Kong   Karachi
Kuala Lumpur   Madrid   Melbourne   Mexico City   Nairobi
New Delhi   Shanghai   Taipei   Toronto

With offices in
Argentina   Austria   Brazil   Chile   Czech Republic   France   Greece
Guatemala   Hungary   Italy   Japan   Poland   Portugal   Singapore
South Korea   Switzerland   Thailand   Turkey   Ukraine   Vietnam

Published by Oxford University Press, Inc.
198 Madison Avenue, New York, NY 10016
www.oup.com

ISBN-13: 978-0-19-522323-1 (California edition)   ISBN-13: 978-0-19-518887-5

Writer: Scott Ingram
Project Manager: Matt Fisher
Project Director: Jacqueline A. Ball
Education Consultant: Diane L. Brooks, Ed.D.
Design: designlabnyc

Casper Grathwohl, Publisher

Printed in the United States of America
on acid-free paper

Dear Parents, Guardians, and Students:

This study guide has been created to increase student enjoyment and understanding of
A History of US.

The study guide offers a wide variety of interactive exercises to support every chapter. At
the back of the guide are maps to help tie the study of history to the study of geography.
(Corresponding activities appear in the teaching guide for this book.) Also at the back of
the guide are several copies of a library/media center research log students can use to
organize research projects and assignments. Parents or other family members can
participate in activities marked "With a Parent or Partner." Adults can help in other ways,
too. One important way is to encourage students to create and use a history journal as
they work through the exercises in the guide. The journal can simply be an off-the-shelf
notebook or three-ring binder used only for this purpose. Some students might like to
customize their journals with markers, colored paper, drawings, or computer graphics. No
matter what it looks like, a journal is a student's very own place to organize thoughts,
practice writing, and make notes on important information. It will serve as a personal
report of ongoing progress that your child's teacher can evaluate regularly. When
completed, it will be a source of satisfaction and accomplishment for your child.

Sincerely,

Casper Grathwohl
Publisher

This book belongs to:

_____

CONTENTS

to the detriment of the natural ecosystem. A pioneer's daughter describes in vivid detail the adventures of a trip through the wet prairie in a covered wagon.

Library/Media Center Research Log
Map Resource Pages

HOW TO USE THE
STUDENT STUDY GUIDES TO
A HISTORY OF US

One word describes A History of US: stories. Every book in this series is packed with stories about people who built a brand new country like none before. You will meet presidents and politicians, artists and inventors, ordinary people who did amazing things and had wonderful adventures. The best part is that all the stories are true. All the people are real.

As you read this book, you can enjoy the stories while you build valuable thinking and writing skills. The book will help you pass important tests. The sample pages below show special features in all the History of US books. Take a look!

Before you read

- Have a notebook or extra paper and a pen handy to make a history journal. A dictionary and thesaurus will help you too.

- Read the chapter title and predict what you will learn from the chapter. Note that often the author often adds humor to her titles with plays on words or **puns**, as in this title.

- Study all maps, photos, and their captions closely. The captions often contain important information you won't find in the text.

A HISTORY OF US

27 Howe Billy Wished France Wouldn't Join In

General Howe had already served in America. In 1759 he led Wolfe's troops to seize Quebec.

A **hoop-stay** was part of the stiffening in a skirt; a **jupon** was part of a corset. **Matrons** are married women. The **misses** are single girls; **swains** and **beaux** are young men or boyfriends. **Making love** meant flirting. **British Grenadiers** are part of the royal household's infantry.

Sir William Howe (who was sometimes called Billy Howe) was in charge of all the British forces in America. It was Howe who drove the American army from Long Island to Manhattan. Then he chased it across another river to New Jersey. And, after that, he forced George Washington to flee on—to Pennsylvania. It looked as if it was all over for the rebels. In New Jersey, some 3,000 Americans took an oath of allegiance to the king. But Washington got lucky again. The Europeans didn't like to fight in cold weather.

Sir William settled in New York City for the winter season. Howe thought Washington and his army were done for and could be

Swarming with Beaux

Rebecca Franks was the daughter of a wealthy Philadelphia merchant. Her father was the king's agent in Pennsylvania, and the family were Loyalists. Rebecca visited New York when it was occupied by the British. Her main interest in the war was that it meant New York was full of handsome officers:

My Dear Abby, By the by, few New York ladies know how to entertain company in their own houses unless they introduce the card tables....I don't know a woman or girl that can chat above half an hour, and that on the form of a cap, the colour of a ribbon or the set of a hoop-stay or jupon....Here, you enter a room with a formal set curtsey and after the how do's, 'tis a fine, or a bad day, and those trifling nothings are finish'd, all's a dead calm till the cards are in- troduced, when you see pleasure dancing in the eyes of all the matrons....The misses, if they have a favorite swain, frequently decline playing for the pleasure of making love....Yesterday the Grenadiers had a race at the Flatlands, and in the afternoon this house swarm'd with beaux and some very smart ones. How the girls wou'd have envy'd me cou'd they have peep'd and seen how I was surrounded.

126

As you read

- Keep a list of questions.

- Note the bold-faced definitions in the margins. They tell you the meanings of important words and terms – ones you may not know.

- Look up other unfamiliar words in a dictionary.

- Note other sidebars or special features. They contain additional information for your enjoyment and to build your understanding. Often sidebars and features contain quotations from primary source documents such as a diary or letter, like this one. Sometimes the primary source item is a cartoon or picture.

finished off in springtime. Besides, Billy Howe loved partying. And some people say he liked the Americans and didn't approve of George III's politics. For reasons that no one is quite sure of, General Howe just took it easy.

But George Washington was no quitter. On Christmas Eve of 1776, in bitter cold, Washington got the Massachusetts fishermen to ferry his men across the Delaware River from Pennsylvania back to New Jersey. The river was clogged with huge chunks of ice. You had to be crazy, or coolly courageous, to go out into that dangerous water. The Hessians, on the other side—at Trenton, New Jersey— were so sure Washington wouldn't cross in such bad weather that they didn't patrol the river. Washington took them by complete surprise.

A week later, Washington left a few men to tend his campfires and fool the enemy. He quietly marched his army to Prince-ton, New Jersey, where he surprised and beat a British force. People in New Jersey forgot the oaths they had sworn to the king. They were Patriots again.

Those weren't big victories that Washington had won, but they certainly helped American morale. And American morale needed help. It still didn't seem as if the colonies had a chance. After all, Great Britain had the most feared army in the world. It was amazing that a group of small colonies would even attempt to fight the powerful British empire. When a large English army (9,500 men and 138 cannons) headed south from Canada in June 1777, many observers thought the rebellion would soon be over.

The army was led by one of Britain's

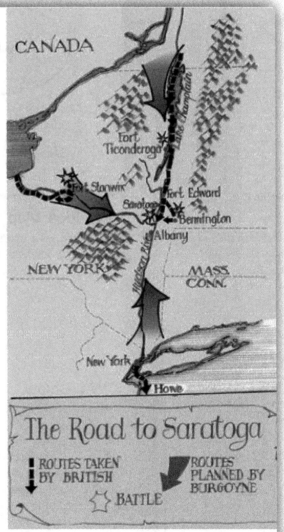

The Road to Saratoga

↕ ROUTES TAKEN BY BRITISH

↘ ROUTES PLANNED BY BURGOYNE

☆ BATTLE

General Burgoyne's redcoats carried far too much equipment. Each man's boots alone weighed 12 pounds. They took two months to cover 40 miles from Fort Ticonderoga to Saratoga, and lost hundreds of men to American snipers.

127

After you read

- Compare what you have learned with what you thought you would learn before you began the chapter.

The next two pages have models of graphic organizers. You will need these to do the activities for each chapter on the pages after that. Go back to the book as often as you need to.

GRAPHIC ORGANIZERS

As you read and study history, geography, and the social sciences, you'll start to collect a lot of information. Using a graphic organizer is one way to make information clearer and easier to understand. You can choose from different types of organizers, depending on the information.

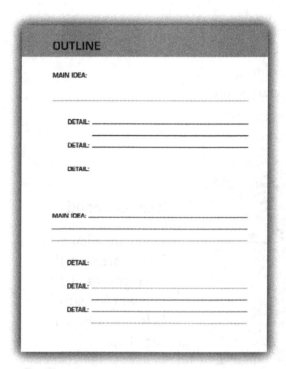

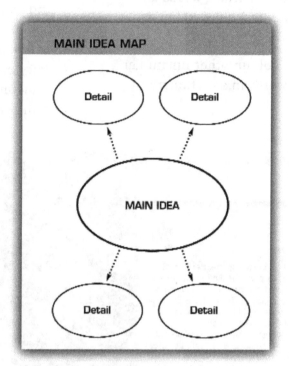

Outline

To build an outline, first identify your main idea. Write this at the top. Then, in the lines below, list the details that support the main idea. Keep adding main ideas and details as you need to.

Main Idea Map

Write down your main idea in the central circle. Write details in the connecting circles.

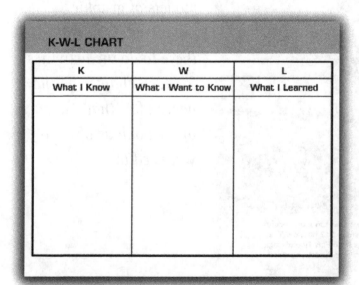

K-W-L Chart

Before you read a chapter, write down what you already know about a subject in the left column. Then write what you want to know in the center column. Then write what you learned in the last column. You can make a two-column version of this. Write what you know in the left and what you learned after reading the chapter.

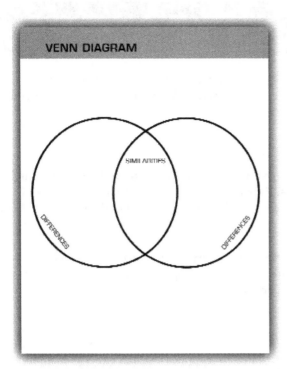

Venn Diagram

These overlapping circles show differences and similarities among topics. Each topic is shown as a circle. Any details the topics have in common go in the areas where those circles overlap. List the differences where the circles do not overlap.

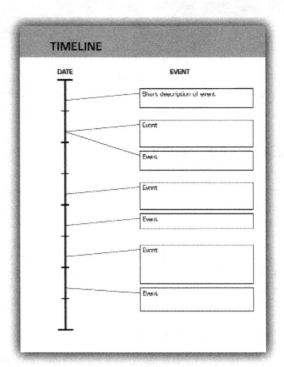

Timeline

A timeline divides a time period into equal chunks of time. Then it shows when events happened during that time. Decide how to divide up the timeline. Then write events in the boxes to the right when they happened. Connect them to the date line.

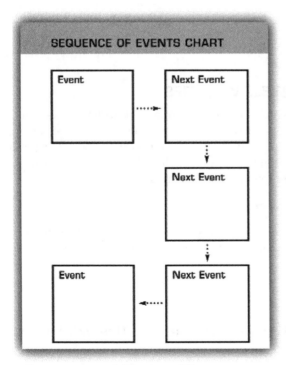

Sequence of Events Chart

Historical events bring about changes. These result in other events and changes. A sequence of events chart uses linked boxes to show how one event leads to another, and then another.

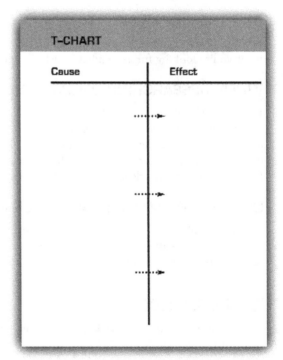

T–Chart

Use this chart to separate information into two columns. To separate causes and effects, list events, or causes, in one column. In the other column, list the change, or effect, each event brought about.

REPORTS AND SPECIAL PROJECTS

Aside from the activities in this Study Guide, your teacher may ask you to do some extra research or reading about American history on your own. Or, you might become interested in a particular story you read in *A History of US* and want to find out more. Do you know where to start?

GETTING STARTED

The back of every History of US book has a section called "More Books to Read." Some of these books are fiction and some are nonfiction. This list is different for each book in the series. When you want to find out more about a particular topic from the reading, these books are a great place to start—and you should be able to find all of them in your school library.

Also, if you're specifically looking for *primary sources*, you can start with the *History of US Sourcebook and Index*. This book is full of *primary sources*, words and evidence about history directly from the people who were involved. This is an excellent place to find the exact words from important speeches and documents.

DOING RESEARCH

For some of the group projects and assignments in this course, you will need to conduct research either in a library or online. When your teacher asks you to research a topic, remember the following tips:

TO FIND GOOD EVIDENCE, START WITH GOOD SOURCES

Usually, your teacher will expect you to support your research with *primary sources*. Remember that a primary source for an event comes from someone who was there when the event took place. The best evidence for projects and writing assignments always comes from *primary sources,* so if you can't seem to find any right away, keep looking.

ASK THE LIBRARIAN

Librarians are amazing people who can help you find just about anything in the library. If you can't seem to find what you're looking for, remember to ask a librarian for help.

WHEN RESEARCHING ONLINE, STICK TO CREDIBLE WEBSITES

It can be difficult to decide which websites are credible and which are not. To be safe, stick with websites that both you and your teacher trust. There are plenty of online sources that have information you can trust to be correct, and usually they're names you already know. For example, you can trust the facts you get from places like pbs.org, census.gov, historychannel.com, and historyofus.com. In addition to free websites like these, check with your librarian to see which *databases and subscription-based websites* your school can access.

USE THE LIBRARY/MEDIA CENTER RESEARCH LOG

At the back of this study guide, you'll find several copies of a Library/Media Center Research Log. Take one with you to the library or media center, and keep track of your sources. Also, take time to decide how helpful and relevant those sources are.

OTHER RESOURCES

Your school and public library have lots of additional resources to help you with your research. These include videos, DVDs, software, and CDs.

CARNEGIE

SUMMARY *Andrew Carnegie's life went from rags to riches. He put his altruistic ideals on hold while he amassed his wealth. Then in the last third of his life, he changed from robber baron to philanthropist, giving away more than 90 percent of his fortune to civic projects.*

ACCESS

A good graphic organizer for these chapters is the main idea map on page 8. Copy the diagram in your history journal. In the largest circle, write the words *Andrew Carnegie*. Use each of the circles to write facts about Carnegie from childhood to old age.

WORD BANK   alloy   benefactor   Morse Code   Bessemer process   strike   capital   pollution

Complete the sentences below with words from the word bank. One word is not used.

1. Steel was an _____, or a mixture of elements, that was made cheaply through the _____ that was originally developed by William Kelly.

2. A _____ is a person who gives money or jobs to people.

3. _____ was a system of dots and dashes used to communicate over the telegraph.

4. _____ is another name for money.

5. A _____ occurs when workers walk off of their jobs.

CRITICAL THINKING SEQUENCE OF EVENTS

The events below describe the life of Andrew Carnegie. Put 1, 2, 3, and so on to put the sentences in chronological order.

_____   A year later he heard that a messenger boy was needed at the new telegraph office in Pittsburgh.

_____   "Good heavens," declared Carnegie. "Where did I get all that money?"

_____   But when the Industrial Revolution came to Scotland, Andrew's father could find no work.

_____   His first job in Allegheny, Pennsylvania, was as a bobbin boy in a textile factory.

_____   Carnegie became king of America's steel industry, and soon American steel dominated the world.

_____   When salaries were cut at Carnegie's Homestead steel mill, in Pennsylvania, the workers went on strike.

_____   Carnegie invested in railroads, railroad sleeping cars, bridges, and oil derricks; by age 33, he was rich.

_____   Then the most successful banker in America, J. Pierpont Morgan, offered to buy Carnegie out.

WORKING WITH PRIMARY SOURCES

Read the words of Hamlin Garland below. In your history journal, write complete sentences to answer the questions.

> The streets were horrible; the buildings poor; the sidewalks sunken and full of holes. . . . Everywhere the yellow mud of the streets lay kneaded into sticky masses through which groups of pale, lean men slouched in faded garments.

1. Why would it be difficult to walk to work in a steel town?

2. What do you think the word "kneaded" means in the statement above?

3. From reading the words above, why do you think the men "slouched" through the "yellow mud"?

4. What do you think the men are "pale" and "lean"?

WRITING

Look at the illustrations of factory workers in the chapter. What words would you use to describe their working conditions? In your history journal, describe a day in the life of a factory worker.

2 A BOOKKEEPER NAMED ROCKEFELLER

SUMMARY *John D. Rockefeller streamlined the process of oil refining and transport, creating a monopoly through his company, Standard Oil. His often unscrupulous business dealings taught the nation hard lessons about the unbridled power of capitalism.*

ACCESS

A good graphic organizer for these chapters is the main idea map on page 8. Copy the diagram in your history journal. In the largest circle, write the word *Rockefeller*. Use each of the circles to write facts about his life.

WORD BANK   rebate   kickback   monopoly   capitalism   internal combustion   gusher

Complete the sentences below with words from the word bank. One word is not used.

1. When railroads paid back money to Rockefeller that he had paid to ship his oil, it was called a

   _____ or a _____.

2. The _____ engine had not been invented when Rockefeller made his
   money from oil.

3. Rockefeller had complete control, otherwise known as a _____, on the oil industry.

4. In the economic system known as _____, people can use money to make money.

CRITICAL THINKING FACT OR OPINION

A fact is a statement that can be proven. An opinion judges things or people, but cannot be proved or disproved. Put F or O in front of the sentences below from the chapter.

_____ 1. In 1858, a small-time prospector named Edwin Drake sank a hole 70 feet into the ground near Titusville, Pennsylvania.

_____ 2. Rockefeller began buying his competitors.

_____ 3. Rockefeller's bookkeeper mind seemed interested only in money and profits, not in people.

_____ 4. When some miners tried to form unions, Rockefeller shut the mines and actually let the miners starve.

_____ 5. Rockefeller claimed he didn't know what was going on—but he did.

_____ 6. The Bible and his mother's teaching made Rockefeller generous.

_____ 7. Rockefeller lived until 1937; he was 98 when he died.

WORKING WITH PRIMARY SOURCES

Read a friend's description of Rockefeller below. In your history journal, answer the questions that follow with complete sentences.

   Mad about money though sane in everything else.

1. How is word "mad" used in the statement above?

2. How would someone who was "mad about money" act?

3. How does the word "sane" help you understand the meaning of the word "mad"?

4. What do you think the friend meant by "everything else"?

MR. STORYTELLER

SUMMARY *Lyman Frank Baum softened the hard edges of the Gilded Age through whimsical children's stories that showed the follies of conflict and the virtues of gentleness.*

ACCESS

This chapter discusses a famous author of children's books, L. Frank Baum. In your history journal, make a cause and effect chart (see the T-chart on page 9). For the first cause, write *Baum was often sick as a child.* List the effect. What was the cause that resulted from the first effect? Fill in at least five cause-and-effect relationships with information from the chapter.

WORD BANK   satire

Find the page on which the word above appears. In a dictionary, look up the word. Rewrite the sentence in the chapter in which the word appears using the definition.

CRITICAL THINKING DRAWING CONCLUSIONS

Each of the sentences in *italics* below is taken from the chapter. Put a check mark in front of all of the conclusions that can be drawn from reading the lines.

1. *He was a gentle boy, often sick, who had to stay home from school and couldn't play ball games with other boys.*

_____ (a) Baum spent a great deal of time alone.

_____ (b) Baum was not as strong as other boys his age.

_____ (c) None of the other boys liked Baum.

2. *Baum grew up and went to work and tried to be serious.*

_____ (a) Baum was an aggressive, hard-working businessman.

_____ (b) Baum did not enjoy being serious.

_____ (c) Baum did not fit in with other working men.

3. *He told stories about people he made up, but his characters all became real in his mind.*

_____ (a) Baum had a good imagination.

_____ (b) Baum had mental problems.

_____ (c) Making up stories was easy for Baum.

HISTORY JOURNAL

Don't forget to share your history journal with your classmates, and ask if you can see what their journals look like. You might be surprised—and get some new ideas.

POWERFUL PIERPONT

SUMMARY *J. P. Morgan commanded a financial empire with the power to bail out federal and city governments. Morgan's skillful wielding of investment capital enabled him to build the nation's first billion-dollar corporation. Morgan was to banking what Carnegie was to steel and Rockefeller was to oil.*

MONOPOLY—NOT ALWAYS A GAME

SUMMARY *Monopolies put the "big" into big business. But they also threatened the competition that fuels a market economy. This situation created a dilemma: Could the federal government regulate business without crushing the spirit of capitalism?*

ACCESS

To help understand these chapters on banker J.P. Morgan and monopolies, make a K-W-L graphic organizer in your history journal like the one on page 8. In the "What I Know" column write what you have learned so far about big business in the late 1800s. In the "What I Want to Know" column, write five questions you have about monopolies and banks. After you read the chapters, fill out the "What I Learned" column with answers to your questions and other information.

WORD BANK   bankrupt   trustees   corruption   liability   corporation

Complete the sentences below with words from the word bank. One word is not used.

1. A person, company, city, or state that does not have enough money to meet its expenses is _____.

2. _____ are people who manage large organizations such as universities or corporations.

3. _____ is widespread crime among business or political leaders.

4. A _____ is a responsibility for money that is owed or products that are made.

CRITICAL THINKING MAIN IDEA AND SUPPORTING DETAILS

Each sentences in italics below states a main idea from the chapters. Put a check mark in the blanks in front of the ONE sentence that DOES NOT support or tell more about the main idea.

1. *J.P. Morgan was not like Andrew Carnegie.*

_____ (a) Morgan did not start as a poor boy and work his way to riches.

_____ (b) But J.P. was very rich and very powerful, and vain and arrogant, too.

_____ (c) Morgan started at the top.

2. *By the beginning years of the new century, the House of Morgan (the name of J.P.'s bank) could be found in almost every important field of American business.*

_____ (a) The bank controlled railroads, shipping, the manufacture of agricultural tools, telephones, telegraphs, electrical power, insurance, and city transportation.

_____ (b) Remember, it was J. Pierpont Morgan who bought Andrew Carnegie's steel company.

_____ (c) "The great monopoly in this country is the money monopoly," said Morgan.

3. *Regulating business in a capitalist country is not easy.*

_____ (a) Most businesspeople want as little regulation as possible.

_____ (b) But the public needs to be protected from unfair business practices.

_____ (c) A trust is a legal arrangement that allows many different companies to be owned and run by the same people.

WORKING WITH PRIMARY SOURCES

Study the cartoon of the "monopoly octopus" on page 33. What industries are shown on the tentacles of the octopus? Why are those industries important? Which are still important today? What do you think is the opinion of the cartoonist about monopolies?

BUILDERS AND DREAMERS

SUMMARY *While tycoons changed the conduct of business, architects and engineers changed the urban landscape of America. Their fierce individualism created innovations destined to become world famous.*

ACCESS

To help understand this important chapter that describes the people and objects in this chapter, make an outline like the one on page 8. For the title, write *Builders and Dreamers*. List the men in the chapter as main ideas. Put at least two details under each main idea.

WORD BANK   innovation   suspension   architect   cantilever cable   skyscraper   culture

Complete the sentences below with words from the word bank. One word is not used.

1. An _____ is needed to design a _____ or a tall building before it is built.

2. A _____ bridge is hung across water with wire rope, or _____.

3. An _____ is new idea.

4. A steel _____ is built to connect a bridge from opposite sides of a waterway.

CRITICAL THINKING   MAKING INFERENCES

Put a B in front of each sentence below that is about a bridge. Put a P in front of each sentence that is about a park. Put an S in front of each sentences that is about a skyscraper.

_____   He made formal areas with fountains, playgrounds, and concert shells.

_____   Then James Eads designed three steel arches and sank them into the Mississippi.

_____   He created wild and rugged areas.

_____   Nature had a lot of help from Frederick Olmstead.

_____   The stone towers needed to anchor the steel rope could not be placed on land.

_____   Thick walls weren't needed to support the building.

_____   Rivers needed to be crossed.

WORKING WITH PRIMARY SOURCES

Read the words of Frederick Olmstead below. In your history journal, answer the questions that follow.

> Plant spacious parks in your cities, and unloose their gates as wide as the gate of morning to the whole people.

1. What does the word "plant" mean in the sentence above?

2. What does Olmstead mean when he says that parks should "unloose their gates"?

3. How does he compare a park to the sky?

4. Who does he mean when he says "the whole people"?

WRITING

Imagine that you are one of the builders and dreamers described in the chapter. If you were asked to design something for your neighborhood, what would you create? In your history journal, make a plan or drawing for an impressive building, park, or structure for your town.

CHAPTER 7

LADY L

SUMMARY *The greatest enemy of monopolies and unbridled power by the few has always been the American belief in individual rights. In 1885, the people of France honored this belief by presenting the American people with the Statue of Liberty—a worldwide symbol of freedom and opportunity.*

ACCESS

To organize the information in this chapter, make a timeline graphic organizer in your history journal like the one on page 9. Begin in the year 1865 (what happened then?) and locate all of the other dates you can find in the chapter. Write down facts that you learn about what happened in each year. Can you determine from the information in the chapter when the Statue of Liberty was opened to the public?

WORD BANK
icon   sonnet   pogrom   golden door   philosopher

Complete the sentences below with words from the word bank. One word is not used.

1. An _____ is an object that is a symbol of a nation, a religion, or an idea.

2. Emma Lazarus used the term _____ to mean the entry to America in her poem, a

   _____ titled "The New Colossus."

3. _____ is the term used to refer to massacre of Jews in the 1800s.

CRITICAL THINKING SEQUENCE OF EVENTS

The sentences from the chapter below describe the events in the chapter. Put 1, 2, 3, and so on to put the sentences in chronological order.

_____ Eiffel designed a skeleton of iron bars.

_____ Bartholdi began work in his studio, but the great statue soon outgrew that home.

_____ When he sailed to New York, Bartholdi was struck by the beauty and openness of its harbor.

_____ But when Liberty was finished she needed a place to stand.

_____ All across America, people began to respond.

_____ Edouard de Laboulaye, the scholarly host at that dinner, was talking about liberty and America.

_____ The last five lines of Lazarus's poem are engraved on the pedestal of the statue.

WORKING WITH PRIMARY SOURCES

Read the words from the *New York World* below. In your history journal, answer the questions that follow.

> It is not a gift from the millionaires of France to the millionaires of America, but a gift of the whole people of France to the whole people of America.

1. To what "gift" does the editorial refer?

2. Does the paper think the gift would be less meaningful if millionaires gave it? Why or why not?

3. What does the term "whole people" mean?

4. How do the "whole people" of one country give a "gift" to another country?

PRESIDENTS AGAIN

SUMMARY *Nine presidents held office between the end of the Civil War and the turn of the 20th century. Some were capable leaders, but most could not solve the new problems the nation faced.*

ACCESS

This chapter discusses the presidents who served from 1865 to 1900. In your history journal, make a timeline divided into five-year periods. Write the name of each president in the section of the timeline during which he served.

WORD BANK   Civil Service   Jim Crow   anarchist   Sherman Antitrust Act   temperance   assassin

Complete the sentences below with words from the word bank. One word is not used.

1. An _____ is someone who does not believe in any form of government.

2. In the South, the laws that discriminated against black people were called _____ laws.

3. Many people supported a _____ movement to ban the use of alcohol.

4. The _____ kept businesses from becoming too powerful.

5. The _____ was the name given to the organization of people who worked for the U.S. government.

CRITICAL THINKING FACT OR OPINION

A fact is a statement that can be proven. An opinion judges things or people, but cannot be proved or disproved. Put F or O in front of the sentences from the chapter below from the chapter.

_____ 1. Some of these presidents were stronger than they may seem.

_____ 2. It probably would have been better for the country if someone else had been vice president when Lincoln was shot.

_____ 3. During the Johnson and Grant presidencies, Congress sent troops south to see that elections were open to everyone.

_____ 4. President and Mrs. Hayes set a good example.

_____ 5. The Civil Service Commission made people take examinations for government jobs.

_____ 6. There was too much money in the Treasury!

_____ 7. Inside, in a specially equipped operating room, surgeons removed two teeth and the cancer.

_____ 8. When Roosevelt took office, the time of weak presidents was over.

WORKING WITH PRIMARY SOURCES

Read the words from *Puck* that describe Lucy Hayes. Answer the questions that follow.

How wine her tender spirit riles, while water wreathes her face in smiles.

1. From reading the chapter, what do you know about Lucy Hayes?

2. What does the word "riles" mean in the sentence above?

3. Does Lucy Hayes have a "tender spirit" about wine?

4. What does the work "wreathes" mean in the sentence above?

WRITING

In your history journal, write sentence that is better than "Joe Got His Gun And Chased His Crazy Mule" on page 56 to help you remember the names of the presidents.

THE PEOPLE'S PARTY

SUMMARY *Changing economic conditions brought hard times to the nation's farmers in the late 1880s. Angered by the failure of government to help them, many farmers backed a new political party that promised economic aid and greater democracy.*

ACCESS

This chapter describes the rise of a political party that addressed the needs of poor people, especially farmers. To help understand the importance of farmers in the political issues of the time make a K-W-L graphic organizer in your history journal like the one on page 8. In the "What I *Know*" column write what you know about the farming after the Civil War. (If you don't know anything, that's OK.) In the "What I *Want* to Know" column, write three questions you have about the farmers. After you read the chapter, fill out the "What I *Learned*" column with answers to your questions and other information.

WORD BANK   graduated income tax   agitator   combine   suffrage   mortgages

Complete the sentences below with words from the word bank. One word is not used.

1. An _____ is someone who stirs up trouble.

2. Women's _____, the right to vote, was an important issue for many people.

3. The _____ was a plan under which wealthy people paid more to the government than poor people.

4. A _____ is a large piece of farm equipment that harvests wheat.

MAP

Find the modern U.S. political map in the atlas section of your book and compare it to the map on page 59.

1. What states in the United States are shown on the map? _____

2. What area of the country is the *Cotton Belt*? _____

3. What area of the country is the *Corn Belt"* _____

4. What area of the country is the *Hay and Pasture*? _____

CRITICAL THINKING MAIN IDEA AND SUPPORTING DETAILS

Each sentence in *italics* below states a main idea from the chapter. Put a check mark in the blanks in front of the ONE sentence that DOES NOT support or tell more about the main idea.

1. *Those reformers spoke for ordinary Americans who didn't want to be left out of the good times that were being enjoyed by others.*

_____ (a) The Democrats have become the only party with power in the South.

_____ (b) They demanded rights.

_____ (c) They were just people who wanted to take part in the governing process.

2. *The Populist leaders tell the farmers there is a conspiracy.*

_____ (a) They say the eastern bankers, the railroad magnates, and the grain elevator operators are plotting against them.

_____ (b) Some people are calling this time "the gay nineties."

_____ (c) They are keeping the farmers poor so they can get richer.

3. *Before the Civil War, life seemed simpler.*

_____ (a) Most people, then, were farmers who grew their own food, spun their own yarn, chopped their own timber, and had to buy little outside.

_____ (b) Now farming has changed.

_____ (c) They sat on red damask chairs and dug with silver shovels in a play sandbox filled with rubies and diamonds.

MAKING MONEY

SUMMARY *A shortage of money in circulation added the economic woes of farmers and poor people. Through populist leaders, they pushed for a democratically controlled monetary system.*

ACCESS

This chapter gives basic information about money in the late 1800s. Copy the main idea map from page 8 into your history journal. In the large circle, write *Money*. In the smaller circles, write facts about the money as you read them.

WORD BANK

inflation   gold standard   greenback   deflation   Federal Reserve   specie   surplus

Complete the sentences below with words from the word bank. One word is not used.

1. _____ is a rise in prices due to an increase in the amount of money in circulation.

2. During the Civil War, a _____ was a note from the government, but was not backed by _____, or "real" metal money.

3. A _____ backs up all paper money with gold.

4. The _____ was a government-supported banking program favored by Populists.

5. _____ is a drop in prices due to a shrinking amount of money in circulation.

CRITICAL THINKING MAKING INFERENCES

Put I if the sentence below describes inflation. Put D if the sentence describes deflation.

_____ 1. When there's no demand, prices drop until goods are cheap enough for people to start buying them again.

_____ 2. The people selling the goods put their prices up.

_____ 3. It takes more money to buy something than it did before.

_____ 4. There isn't much money to pay for things, so people can't sell them.

_____ 5. The more dollars there are in circulation, the less each dollar is worth.

_____ 6. There is less money around.

WORKING WITH PRIMARY SOURCES

Read the words from the caption on page 65 that accompanies the anti-greenback comic strip. In your history journal, answer the questions that follow.

> The great experimental money doctor succeeds in making a rag baby; "Bless its dear little heart, it is as good as Gold!' But the little pet grows rapidly, and becomes too heavy to carry; the creature arises and pursues its parent, and—The End.

1. Who do you think "the great experimental doctor" is?

2. Why is the "rag baby" "as good as Gold" at first?

3. What is the name for the economic condition that resulted when "the little pet grows rapidly, and becomes too heavy"?

4. Who are the creature's "parents"?

IN YOUR OWN WORDS

In your history journal, rewrite the four steps in the comic on page 65 in your own words.

HARD TIMES

SUMMARY *A tight supply of money spawned a financial panic in 1893. Following that panic came one of the worst depressions ever.*

GOLD AND SILVER

SUMMARY *As Americans suffered through the depression, the question of whether the nation's money should be backed by gold alone or by a combination of gold and silver became a hot topic.*

ACCESS

These chapters describe economic difficulties faced by many Americans during the 1890s. To help understand the information in these chapters, make a K-W-L graphic organizer in your history journal like the one on page 8. In the "What I Know" column write what you know about poverty in the late 1800s. (If you don't know anything, that's OK.) In the "What I Want to Know" column, write three questions you have about poverty in the late 1800s. After you read the chapter, fill out the "What I Learned" column with answers to your questions and other information.

WORD BANK   mortgage   installment   default   foreclose   scab   assay office   droughts

Complete the sentences below with words from the word bank. One word is not used.

1. People who discovered gold dust took it to an _____ to have it weighed.

2. A _____ is a person who takes the place of a striking worker.

3. A _____ is an amount of money that is loaned to a person and which is repaid in a monthly

   payment called an _____.

4. People who _____, or fail to pay, a monthly fee, may see the bank _____ or take over their property.

CRITICAL THINKING DRAWING CONCLUSIONS

The sentences below in *italics* are taken from the chapter. Put a check mark in front of all of the conclusions that can be drawn from reading the lines.

1. *Unemployment in 1894 is said to have been higher, in relation to the country's population, than at any time in our history.*

_____ (a) A large percentage of workers did not have jobs in 1894.

_____ (b) More people were unemployed in 1894 than at any time in our history

_____ (c) Even though more people were unemployed in later years, unemployment affected a larger part of the overall population in 1894 than at later times.

2. *President Cleveland didn't believe it was his job to do anything about the unemployed.*

_____ (a) There were no unemployment departments in the late 1800s.

_____ (b) Cleveland was a corrupt president.

_____ (c) The responsibilities of government were different in the 1800s than they are today.

3. *But many Americans thought it was humiliating for the president of the United States to have to go to a private banker for help.*

_____ (a) Private bankers had more gold than the U.S. government.

_____ (b) Many Americans expected their leaders to manage the nation's money.

_____ (c) Private bankers got their gold dishonestly.

WRITING

Study the drawing of soldiers and strikers on page 73. Write two captions for the drawing. Make one caption show your support for the strikers. Make the other caption show your support for the soldiers.

A CROSS OF GOLD

SUMMARY *The presidential elections of 1896 pitted William Jennings Bryan against William McKinley, but the race involved more than the two men and their parties. It posed questions about the type and degree of democracy the American people wanted.*

ACCESS

This chapter describes the presidential election of 1896. To organize the information, copy the outline graphic organizer from page 8 into your history journal. For the title, write *Election 1896*. For main ideas, put *Candidates*, *Issues*, *Campaign*, and *Result*. Write at least two details under each main idea.

WORD BANK   constituents   special interest group   whistle stop   delegates

Complete the sentences below with words from the word bank. One word is not used.

1. Another name for the people an official represents is _____.

2. Wealthy people who can persuade a candidate of their views are often part of a _____.

3. Bryan went on a _____ campaign, traveling by train around the country.

CRITICAL THINKING MAIN IDEA AND SUPPORTING DETAILS

Each sentences in *italics* below states a main idea from the chapter. Put a check mark in the blanks in front of the ONE sentence that DOES NOT support or tell more about the main idea.

1. *The Democratic convention gathered in a packed auditorium in Chicago.*
_____ (a) The delegates were to pick a candidate for president.
_____ (b) Bryan went to the Library of Congress, got books, read them, thought about gold and silver, and formed opinions.
_____ (c) Few even considered the young man from Nebraska—until he got up to speak about silver.

2. *In the meantime, the Republicans chose an Ohioan, William McKinley, as their candidate.*
_____ (a) Populists should have their own candidate.
_____ (b) He looked distinguished and presidential.
_____ (c) He was conservative and moderate.

3. *Bryan had little money for his campaign, but he had remarkable energy and that mellifluous voice.*
_____ (a) Sometimes he spoke 30 times a day.
_____ (b) The election of 1896 was one of the most important in our nation's history.
_____ (c) Often he talked from a platform at the end of the train.

WORKING WITH PRIMARY SOURCES

Read the words of Willa Cather below. In your history journal, answer the questions that follow.

> There, with an audience of . . . bronzed farmers who believed in him as their deliverer, the man who could lead them out of . . . debt . . . stay the drought and strike water from the rock, I heard [Bryan] make the speech of his life. . . . I saw those rugged men of the soil weep like children.

1. Why does Cather describe the farmers as "bronzed"?
2. What does phrase "stay the drought" mean in the sentence above?
3. What does the phrase "strike water from the rock" mean?
4. Why do you think Bryan made the farmers "weep like children"?

WRITING

Think back to the chapters you have read so far. If you had lived in the 1870s, would have preferred to live in the city or the country? Explain your choice in your history journal.

SOME BAD IDEAS

SUMMARY *The unsettled conditions that shook the nation in the late 1800s gave rise to more than a new political party. They also helped set off an ugly burst of racism and bigotry.*

ACCESS

This chapter explains the rise of racism and anti-immigration feelings in the 1890s .To organize the information in the chapter, make a K-W-L graphic organizer in your history journal like the one on page 8. In the "What I *Know*" column write what you know about prejudice in the United States during the late 1800s (if you don't know anything, that's OK.) In the "What I *Want* to Know" column, write five questions you have about prejudice. After you read the chapter, fill out the "What I *Learned*" column with answers to your questions and other information.

WORD BANK   bigot   anti-Semitic   nativist   racism   scapegoats   supremacy   immigrant

Complete the sentences below with words from the word bank. One word is not used.

1. A _____ is someone who is prejudiced against people of different religions or races and who

    believes in the _____ of his or her race.

2. Someone who hates Jews is _____.

3. A _____ was an ignorant person in the 1800s who forgot the original ideas that led to the founding of the United States.

4. _____ by whites against African Americans and Asians also became a problem in the 1890s.

5. Many Americans made immigrants into _____, blaming them for the nation's economic problems.

CRITICAL THINKING   FACT OR OPINION

A fact is a statement that can be proven. An opinion judges things or people, but cannot be proved or disproved. Put F or O in front of the sentences below from the chapter.

_____ 1. Bryan went on to run for president again and again and never made it.

_____ 2. It was too bad, since so many Populist ideas were soon accepted by both Republicans and Democrats.

_____ 3. Watson wasn't the only Populist leader to take up bigoted theories.

_____ 4. When he died, the largest bunch of flowers at his funeral came from the Ku Klux Klan.

_____ 5. Actually, the rich industrialists were no different from the poor farmers.

_____ 6. On the West Coast, many citizens were anti-Asian.

_____ 7. Those 19th century bigots—whom we call "nativists"—were ignorant.

WORKING WITH PRIMARY SOURCES

Read the words of Tom Watson below. In your history journal, answer the questions that follow.

> This is not a political fight. . . . It is . . . an uprising of the people. . . . [They] need spokesmen—not leaders—men in the front who will obey, not command.

1. What does the word "uprising" mean in the excerpt above?

2. Who does Watson mean when he writes about "the people"?

3. What is unusual in Watson's belief that "men in the front" should "obey, not command"?

4. Do you think Watson made wrote these words before or after the People's Party failed? Explain.

PRODUCING GOODS

SUMMARY *New products and new ways of selling those products swept across the nation in the late 1800s. They were among the many changes that transformed America from an agrarian to an industrial nation.*

ACCESS

To help understand the information in this chapter, make a cause and effect chart in your history journal like the one on page 9. For the first cause, put *Soldiers needed uniforms during the Civil War*. For the first effect put. Factories made clothes for civilians. Follow up with at least four links in a cause-and-effect chain that led to the development of mail order catalogues.

WORD BANK   civilian   agrarian   merchandise   catalogue

Complete the sentences below with words from the word bank. One word is not used.

1. A _____ is a person who is not in the military.

2. An _____ society is based on farming.

3. Another name for goods is_____.

CRITICAL THINKING DRAWING CONCLUSIONS

The sentences below in *italics* are taken from the chapter. Put a check mark in front of all of the conclusions that can be drawn from reading the lines.

1. *In the cities, new department stores began selling factory-made clothes, shoes, and things for the house and garden*

_____ (a) Department stores got their name from the different goods sold in each areas or departments.

_____ (b) There were no stores before department stores.

_____ (c) Department stores arose between 1865 and 1900.

2. *In 1920, half of all Americans lived in cities or towns.*

_____ (a) Before 1900, most people lived on farms.

_____ (b) Before 1920, there were no cities.

_____ (c) In the early twentieth century, people moved from farms to towns and cities.

3. *A new immigrant could get off the boat at Ellis Island, head for New York or Chicago or Cincinnati, and quickly find a job.*

_____ (a) Immigrants were allowed to work only in New York, Chicago, or Cincinnati.

_____ (b) Immigrants were able to find jobs in many cities.

_____ (c) Immigrants arriving in the United States landed at Ellis Island.

WORKING WITH PRIMARY SOURCES

Read the words of historian Bruce Catton below. In your history journal, answer the questions that follow.

> Say the worst that can be said about the evils of the machine age . . . the brutality with which the factory systems ground men down. . . . the fact remains that what was done here meant . . . a more abundant life for the people."

1. What does Catton mean by the words "evils of the machine age"?

2. What does the word "ground" mean in the excerpt above?

3. What would be an example of "abundant life" that you read about in the chapter?

4. How would you re-state Catton's words in your own words?

WRITING

Study the catalogue on page 91. In your history journal, make an ad for one of the products you see in your own words.

HARVEST AT HAYMARKET

SUMMARY *As American businesses grew larger, owners and managers often looked on workers at just another resource to be exploited. Workers, trying to improve conditions for themselves, organized into unions but faced stuff opposition from business leaders, the government, and much of the public at large.*

ACCESS   This chapter discusses unions, working conditions, and labor unrest in Chicago and other parts of the U.S. in the late 1800s. To organize the information, make an outline like the one on page 8. For the title, write *Labor in America.* For main ideas put *Conditions, Strikes, Violence,* and *Child Labor.* Put at least two details under each main idea.

WORD BANK   plunder   anarchist   scab   socialist   union

Complete the sentences below with words from the word bank. One word is not used.

1. An _____ does not believe in any government at all.

2. A _____ is a worker who takes the place of striking workers.

3. Union leaders believed that owners wanted to _____ workers, or become wealthy underpaying them.

4. A _____ believes that the government should control industries that affected most citizens.

CRITICAL THINKING   MAKING INFERENCES

Put O in front of the statements below if they reflect the point of view of owners. Put W if the statements reflect the point of view of workers..

_____ 1. A union was "a miniature republic; its affairs were every man's affairs."

_____ 2. "Law! What do I care about law? H'aint I got power?"

_____ 3. "Two men with one of these machines can do an average of about three days' work in one."

_____ 4. "There was not a syllable said about anarchism at the Haymarket meeting."

_____ 5. "I believe that . . . the state where one class dominates over another [is] barbaric."

_____ 6. "Hatred and fierce passions have been aroused; and an injury has resulted to our good name."

WORKING WITH PRIMARY SOURCES

The most famous union leader of the last fifty years is undoubtedly Cesar Chavez. He is known for his struggle for farmworkers' rights—so well known that his birthday, March 31, is a state holiday in California. Read the words from Chavez below. In your history journal, answer the questions that follow.

> Violence [against those who oppress us] just hurts those who are already hurt . . . Instead of exposing the brutality of the oppressor, it justifies it.

1. How would Chavez respond to the trial and execution of four men following the Haymarket Square riot?

2. Would you agree with him? Why or why not?

WORKERS, LABOR (AND A TRIANGLE)

SUMMARY *By focusing on improving conditions for workers rather than on transforming American society, immigrant cigarmaker Samuel Gompers provided leadership that helped the labor union movement grow.*

ACCESS

To help understand the importance of labor in the growth of the United States in the late 1800s, make a K-W-L graphic organizer in your history journal like the one on page 8. In the "What I *Know*" column write what you know about the labor unions. In the "What I *Want* to Know" column, write five questions you have about labor unions. After you read the chapter, fill out the "What I *Learned*" column with answers to your questions and other information about unions.

WORD BANK   tenement   sweatshop   craft union   collective bargaining   boycott   negotiate

Complete the sentences below with words from the word bank. One word is not used.

1. An apartment house for poor people was known as a _____.

2. A _____ is a factory that was hot and airless, where workers worked long hours in dirty rooms.

3. A _____ is a refusal to buy a certain product or to use a certain service.

4. _____ occurs when union leaders speak for workers in attempting to gain wage increases and other rights from owners.

CRITICAL THINKING MAIN IDEA AND SUPPORTING DETAILS

Each sentence in *italics* below states a main idea from the chapter. Put a check mark in the blanks in front of the ONE sentence that DOES NOT support or tell more about the main idea.

1. *American labor laws lagged far behind those of almost every other industrial nation.*

_____ (a) No one could accuse Samuel Gompers of being a radical.

_____ (b) Working conditions were often unsafe, factory pay was rarely fair, and workers had few if any benefits.

_____ (c) In 1900, only one American worker in 12 belonged to a union.

2. *Sam Gompers was a practical man.*

_____ (a) He stayed out of politics.

_____ (b) He had only one goal—to improve working conditions in the United States.

_____ (c) While the cigarmakers rolled the tobacco, they liked to have someone read to them.

3. *In earlier days, businesses were small.*

_____ (a) Usually owners and employees worked together.

_____ (b) But in the industrial age, factories grew bigger and more impersonal.

_____ (c) The workers had to strike to get the right to have cold water to drink.

WORKING WITH PRIMARY SOURCES

Read the words of Samuel Gompers below. Answer the questions that follow.

> Show me the country in which there are no strikes, and I will show you that country in which there is no liberty.

1. What does the word "strikes" mean?

2. How does Gompers use the word "liberty"?

3. Would factory owners have agreed or disagreed with Gompers? Explain?

4. Rewrite Gompers' statement in your own words.

ROLLING THE LEAF IN FLORIDA

SUMMARY *Tampa, Florida, became the center of the American cigarmaking industry in the late 1800s. There, men and women created a multicultural industrial community and an immigrant city uncommon for its time.*

CATCHING THE DAY

SUMMARY *The Everglades in southern Florida in the late 19th century was a large subtropical wilderness that humans later interfered with to the detriment of the natural ecosystem. A pioneer's daughter describes in vivid detail the adventures of a trip through the wet prairie in a covered wagon.*

ACCESS

To organize the information, make an outline like on page 8. For the title, write *Florida*. For main ideas put *Cigar Industry*, *Everglades*, *Immigrants*, and *Pioneers*. Put at least two details under each main idea.

WORD BANK

lector boom town *modernista* mutual-aid societies Libre ecosystem pesticides drainage aquifer prairie biological balance canals

Complete the sentences below with words from the word bank. Two words are not used.

1. In Spanish, a _____ is a writer, and a _____ is a reader.

2. Immigrants who came to a fast-growing _____ like Tampa, formed

   _____, organizations that helped other immigrants who arrived after them.

3. The _____, or the relation of all living things, in an

   _____, is a key to having a healthy environment.

3. The _____ or flow of water filled with _____ used to kill insects has polluted

   Florida's underground water reservoir called an _____.

4. A _____ is a wide flat plain.

MAP

Find the "Florida and the Caribbean" map in the back of this study guide. Look at the maps of Florida that are shown on pages 106 and 110. Mark the following places on your map:

Cuba	Jamaica	Haiti
Dominican Republic	Puerto Rico	Miami
Tampa	Everglades	Lake Okeechobee

WORKING WITH PRIMARY SOURCES

Read the words of Marie St. John below. In your history journal, answer the questions that follow.

> South Florida was uninviting to many because of the mosquitoes, panthers, crocodiles, swamps, and wetlands. But these marks of wild country called my father like the legendary siren song.

1. What does the word "uninviting" mean in the sentence above?

2. What are "marks," and what is the "wild country"?

3. What does the word "legendary" mean in the sentence above?

4. Based on what you have read, is a "siren song" inviting or uninviting? Explain.

TELLING IT LIKE IT IS

SUMMARY *People like Mother Jones and the muckrakers helped to bring change to American society by their ceaseless struggle to make the pubic aware of existing problems.*

ACCESS

To organize the information in the chapter, make a cause and effect chart in your history journal. (See the T-chart on page 9.) For the first cause put *Mother Jones's children die.* What was the effect? For another cause, put *Chicago Fire.* What was the effect? Make three more links in a cause-and-effect chain that tell about events in the life of Mother Jones.

WORD BANK   muckraker   humanitarian   plight   homesteading   piecework   inferno   malaria

Complete the sentences below with words from the word bank. One word is not used.

1. A _____ is a caring person who is concerned about the _____, or unfortunate situation, faced by fellow human beings.

2. A _____ was a person who wrote about the problems caused by unregulated businesses such as meatpacking.

3. Some people preferred _____, or farming, over the _____, or hourly labor, of city factories.

4. The Great Chicago Fire was a blazing _____.

CRITICAL THINKING   DRAWING CONCLUSIONS

Each of the sentences in *italics* below is taken from the chapter. Put a check mark in front of all of the conclusions that can be drawn from reading the lines.

1. *"Mother" Jones was a pugnacious little woman, and fearless.*

_____ (a) Mother Jones liked to argue.

_____ (b) Mother Jones had a short temper.

_____ (c) Mother Jones was a violent person.

2. *The police called Mother Jones a public nuisance.*

_____ (a) Some people thought Mother Jones was a pest.

_____ (b) Mother Jones was a criminal.

_____ (c) Mother Jones did not care if she made enemies.

3. *Now, with big factories and modern transportation, people were buying things made far from their homes.*

_____ (a) People had more choices about products they bought in the late 1800s than ever before.

_____ (b) People knew that everything they bought was healthy or safe.

_____ (c) Before the time of factories and modern transportation, many items were "home made."

4. *Writers were writing about the problems of unregulated business.*

_____ (a) The writers were in favor of laws that protected people.

_____ (b) The writers were in favor of laws that protected businesses.

_____ (c) Business owners were not happy with the writers.

BREAD AND ROSES, TOO

SUMMARY *The Industrial Workers of the World, or Wobblies, hoped to unite all workers in one big union. They never came close to achieving that goal, but they did help textile workers of many cultures organize and win a big strike in Lawrence, Massachusetts in 1912.*

ACCESS

This chapter discusses the actions of a labor union in the early 1900s. To organize the information in the chapter, make a main idea map like the one on page 8. In the center, put *Wobblies*. In the smaller circles, write important facts from the chapter that tell more about this group and its accomplishments.

WORD BANK   ordinances   nullification   pilloried   solidarity   malnutrition   Wobblies

Complete the sentences below with words from the word bank. One word is not used.

1. The _____ of a law means that the law is disregarded by citizens.

2. Another name for laws is _____.

3. The workers' union called the _____ traveled to areas around the country to show

   _____, or support, for striking workers.

4. Many of the leaders of strikes were _____, or heavily criticized, by the press, factory owners, and politicians.

CRITICAL THINKING   MAKING INFERENCES

Put W in front of the sentences below that express a point of view that comes from workers. Put O in front of the sentences that express a point of view that comes from owners.

_____ 1. "The way to settle this strike is to shoot down 40 or 50 of them."

_____ 2. The Massachusetts legislature passed a law saying that women and children were not allowed to work more than 54 hours a week.

_____ 3. "We Want Bread and Roses, Too."

_____ 4. In Lawrence, some leading citizens called the strikes un-American and blamed "foreign influences."

_____ 5. "To pay for 54 hours' work the wages of 56 would equivalent to an increase in wages . . ."

_____ 6. "You can hope for no success on any policy of violence . . . violence means the loss of the strike."

_____ 7. " . . . the mills cannot afford to pay."

_____ 8. But they didn't have a real leader . . . so they appealed to the IWW for help.

WORKING WITH PRIMARY SOURCES

Read the words of the Joe Ettor below. Answer the questions that follow.

They cannot weave cloth with bayonets. By all means make the strike as peaceful as possible.

1. Who are "they" in the excerpt above?

2. Who are the people who "weave cloth"?

3. What are "bayonets" and what does the word represent?

4. Write a sentence in your own words expressing the thoughts of Ettor.

WRITING

In your history journal, design a poster supporting or opposing the Wobblies.

22 23 24

THE FOURTH ESTATE

SUMMARY *For a republic to work, a people must be informed. The job of supplying that information belongs to a free press—our "fourth estate" or "fourth branch of government."*

IDA, SAM, AND THE MUCKRAKERS

SUMMARY *The muckrakers developed investigative journalism—a tool that exposed wrongdoing in U.S. society and government.*

A BOON TO THE WRITER

SUMMARY *S.S. McClure made it possible for good writers to earn a living.*

ACCESS

These chapters discuss the important role the press has played in the early years of the nation and its great influence at the beginning of the twentieth century. To organize the information in the chapters, make an outline like the one on page 8. For the main ideas, write the titles of each of the three chapters. Under each title write at least 3 details from the chapter that help describe the most important information from the story.

WORD BANK

censor   abridge   redress   libel   muckraker   investigative journalism
syndicate   idiosyncrasy   ethics   vernacular   advocacy   media

Complete the sentences below with words from the word bank.

1. In Thomas Jefferson's time, a _____ was not a person who prevented material from reaching the public; he or she examined it.

2. The U.S. Constitution states that the government cannot _____, or cut down on, the freedom of the press—which in the modern age of television today is also known as the _____.

3. A _____ was a writer who challenged the _____ or honesty of corporations with magazine articles that were the beginning of _____.

4. A _____ is a special language used by people in a certain field.

5. An _____ is a peculiar habit.

6. A person who sues for _____, or having her reputation damaged, may receive monetary damages,a lso called _____, from a court.

7. People who join an _____ group are joining in to support a certain cause or a point of view.

8. A _____ is an organization that buys articles from writers and sells them to several publications at once.

CRITICAL THINKING   MAIN IDEA AND SUPPORTING DETAILS

Each sentences in *italics* below states a main idea from the chapters. Put a check mark in the blanks in front of the ONE sentence that DOES NOT support or tell more about the main idea.

1. *At the turn of the century, America had unusually difficult problems to solve.*

_____ (a) John Adams tried to curb the press with the Alien and Sedition Acts.

_____ (b) The country was experiencing astonishing growth; industrialization and urbanization; an influx of many different peoples; and excessive government corruption.

_____ (c) People needed to understand these phenomena to be able to deal with them.

2. *Muckrakers were journalists who wrote about wrongs: about injustice, unfairness, and corruption.*

_____ (a) They wrote about city bosses and told how dishonest government cheated citizens of their rights and money.

_____ (b) They wrote about the mighty industrial tycoons, about how some of them broke the law and got away with it, and why that cost the public great sums of money.

_____ (c) Tarbell vowed never to marry—and she never did.

Continued on next page

3. *At age 14, with a dollar in his pocket, Sam McClure left home.*

_____ (a) He was determined to go to high school but he needed work to do it.

_____ (b) Educated women were expected to teach.

_____ (c) He had no winter overcoat, so he ran to school.

4. *Ida Tarbell wasn't the only writer whom S.S. McClure encouraged.*

_____ (a) He had a knack for finding good writers.

_____ (b) His method was to pay writers well and let them do careful lengthy research.

_____ (c) Steffens's boyhood wasn't at all like McClure's.

WORKING WITH PRIMARY SOURCES

Read the words of Ida Tarbell below. In your history journal, answer the questions that follow.

> Mr. Rockefeller has systematically played with loaded dice. . . .Business played in this way loses all its sportsmanlike qualities. It is fit only for tricksters."

1. What does the word "systematically" mean in the sentence above?

2. What does it mean to say someone plays with "loaded dice"?

3. What does the term "sportsmanlike qualities" mean?

4. What is Tarbell's opinion of Rockefeller? Why does she feel that way?

WRITING

Imagine that you are an investigative journalist who works for S.S. McClure. What issue or problem would you want to research? In your history, write a proposal to McClure about a new story you want to research that will uncover corruption or expose unfairness. Be sure to explain why you think the story would be important.

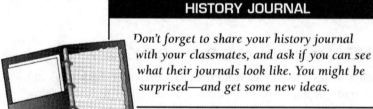

HISTORY JOURNAL

Don't forget to share your history journal with your classmates, and ask if you can see what their journals look like. You might be surprised—and get some new ideas.

IN WILDERNESS IS PRESERVATION

SUMMARY *John Muir used a scientist's eye and a poet's tongue to expose abuses that threatened to deprive Americans of the beauty of their own natural landscape.*

ACCESS

To organize the information in this chapter, make a main idea map in your history journal like the one on page 8. In the center of the organizer put *John Muir*. In the smaller circles, write facts about his life.

WORD BANK   naturalist   habitable   interrelated   extinct

Complete the sentences below with words from the word bank. One word is not used.

1. A _____ is a person who studies plants, animals, water, and land and believes that they are all

   connected, or _____.

2. _____ areas are places in which people can live.

WITH A PARENT OR PARTNER

Look at the map on page 137. With a parent or partner, discuss the following questions. Write your answers in your history journal.

1. Is there a national forest near your town or city?

2. Is there a national park or monument?

3. What forests or parks, if any, have you toured?

4. Discuss the animals that have become extinct. What, do you think, is the reason that so many breeds of wolf became extinct?

WORKING WITH PRIMARY SOURCES

Read the words of John Muir below. Answer the questions that follow.

> Thousands of tired, nerve-shaken, over-civilized people are beginning to find out that . . . wilderness is a necessity, and that . . . parks . . . are . . . not only . . . fountains of time . . . but . . . fountains of life

1. What is the meaning of the word "nerve-shaken" in this passage?

2. What is the meaning of "over-civilized" in this passage?

3. How does Muir use the word "fountain" in two ways?

4. What conclusion can you draw from Muir's words about why he believed that the wilderness should be preserved?

WRITING

In your history journal, design a post card for one of the locations you read about in chapter 25.

THE GILDED AGE TURNS PROGRESSIVE

SUMMARY *A group of reform-minded leaders felt that the problems generated by rapid growth would not correct themselves. Instead they sought progress through governmental action. Their efforts gave birth to the progressive movement.*

ACCESS

In your history journal make a two-circle Venn diagram like the one on page 9. In one circle, write facts about the lives of rich people that you learn from the chapter. In the other circle write facts about the lives of poor people. Try to find at least five facts that you can write in the area where the circles intersect: facts about life in the Gilded Age that affected both rich and poor people.

WORD BANK   activism Progressives direct primary initiative referendum conservatives

Complete the sentences below with words from the word bank. Two words are not used.

1. A _____ allows people to vote in party elections for their candidates for office.

2. _____ were people who believed that government should take action to better the lives of all

   people.

3. An _____ is a request by voter to put a question up to a public vote.

4. A _____ is a vote for or against the question.

CRITICAL THINKING   FACT OR OPINION

A fact is a statement that can be proven. An opinion judges things or people, but cannot be proved or disproved. Put F or O in front of the sentences below from the chapter.

_____ 1. Trains, telephones, electric lights, harvesters, and vacuum cleaners weren't around when the Constitution was written.

_____ 2. Actually, by the year 1900, things were going well for most Americans.

_____ 3. So most Americans had a reason to be optimistic and confident.

_____ 4. Some children—your age—were working 12 to 14 hours a day and not going to school.

_____ 5. Those millions of new people were certainly complicating things.

WORKING WITH PRIMARY SOURCES

Read the words of historian Richard Hofstadter below. Answer the questions that follow.

   Conservatives generally believed in time and nature to bring progress; Progressives believed in energy and governmental action.

1. In what way do Conservatives "conserve" according to the definition above?

2. Who do Progressives look to for "progress"?

3. What makes "time and nature" appeal to Conservatives?

4. Why do "energy" and "action" appeal to Progressives?.

WRITING

Choose one of the photographs on pages 140 and 141 and write a two-sentence caption as though you were a newspaper reporter in the 1900s.

TEEDIE

SUMMARY *The curiosity, energy, and drive of young "Teedie" Roosevelt foreshadowed the vigorous leader who would lead the nation into the 1900s.*

FROM DUDE TO COWBOY

SUMMARY *Roosevelt's adventures in the West left him with an enduring love for the wilderness and a firm belief in nation's destiny to expand.*

ACCESS

These chapters discuss the early life of Theodore Roosevelt. To help organize the information in the chapters, make an outline like the one on page 8. For the title, write *Theodore Roosevelt*. For two main ideas write *childhood* and *young adult*. Write at least two details under each main idea.

WORD BANK   philanthropist idyllic expansionism imperialism specimens

Complete the sentences below with words from the word bank. One word is not used.

1. An _____ life is an ideal or perfect life.

2. Americans who favored growth, or _____, wanted to bring American ideals to countries around the world.

3. Americans who felt that the United States should not force its ideals on other nations spoke out against what they called _____.

4. A _____ is a wealthy person who gives money to causes that benefit society.

CRITICAL THINKING SEQUENCE OF EVENTS

The sentences below describe the events in life of Theodore Roosevelt. Put 1, 2, 3, and so on in front of the sentences that describe what happened

_____   When he became president he surprised people with the wide knowledge he had from books.

_____   And then, on the same day—it was Valentine's Day, 1884—in the same house, Alice died giving birth to a daughter, and Mittie, Theodore's mother, died of typhoid fever.

_____   Teedie pretended he was a Union soldier; his brothers and sisters were not so sure which side to take.

_____   When he went back east, he was ready to accept a new job, as police commissioner of New York.

_____   When he was 14, they spent a winter on a houseboat on the Nile River in Egypt.

_____   The North Dakota cowboys chuckled when the saw the young dude who had come from the East to hunt and become a rancher.

WORKING WITH PRIMARY SOURCES

Read the words of Theodore Roosevelt about a Supreme Court ruling. Answer the questions that follow.

> The judges who rendered this decision . . . knew nothing whatever of tenement-house conditions; they knew legalism, not life. This decision completely blocked . . . reform legislation . . . for a score of years.

1. What does the word "rendered" mean in the passage above?

2. What do you think Roosevelt mean when he says the judges knew "legalism, not life"?

3. How many years is a "score"?

4. Does Roosevelt agree or disagree with the court's decision? How can you tell?

THE SPANISH-AMERICAN WAR

SUMMARY *A war with Spain gave the United States its first taste of foreign empire. Some people relished the new holdings. Others felt that ruling foreign territories demeaned the principles upon which the republic was founded.*

ACCESS

To organize the information in this chapter, make a main idea map in your history journal like the one on page 8. In the center of the organizer put the chapter title the *Spanish-American War*. Fill in smaller circles with facts about the war.

WORD BANK   yellow journalism   archipelago   imperialism

Complete the sentences below with words from the word bank. One word is not used.

1. An _____ is a chain of islands, such as the Philippines.

2. Reporters who make up false stories and report them as if they are true are practicing _____.

WITH A PARENT OR PARTNER

Study the map on page 156.

1. Which possessions did the United States own first?

2. Which possessions does it no longer own?

3. Which possessions have become states?

4. What country could replace "Asia" on the map?

5. Why was the Panama Canal Zone an important possession?

CRITICAL THINKING MAKING INFERENCES

Put A in front of the sentences below if the sentence describes a point of view that is against the Spanish-American War and the Philippines War. Put F is the sentences describes a point of view that is for the Spanish American War and the Philippines War.

_____ 1. [Americans] wanted Spain to clear out of the American hemisphere.

_____ 2. *Assistant Secretary Roosevelt Convinced the Explosion of the War Ship Was Not an Accident*

_____ 3. The newspapers played up the *Maine* story: They called it a Spanish attack.

_____ 4. [William McKinley] knew the horrors of war; he wanted no part of one.

_____ 5. People started calling him a coward.

_____ 6. "We must on no account let the islands go: the American flag is up and it must stay."

_____ 7. Samuel Gompers called it "an unjust war."

_____ 8. Theodore Roosevelt came home from Cuba a hero.

WORKING WITH PRIMARY SOURCES

Read the words of Senator Albert J. Beveridge below. Answer the questions that follow.

Those who do not want the United States to annex foreign lands tell us that we ought not to govern a people without their consent. . . . That rule applies only to . . . people who are capable of self-government.

1. What do you think are "foreign lands" in this passage?

2. What does "govern people without their consent" mean?

3. What is Beveridge's opinion of people in "foreign lands"?

4. Restate Beveridge's thoughts in your own words.

WRITING

In your history journal, write two opinions. One should agree with Beveridge's opinion. The other should disagree, and say that governing people "without their consent" goes against American principles. Write at least three sentences supporting each opinion.

ALOHA OE

SUMMARY *The Hawaiian Islanders lived undisturbed for more than 1,000 years. Soon after outside contact was established, the Hawaiian culture declined. Western missionaries and businesses took control. In 1894, they deposed the queen of Hawaii. In 1898, Hawaii was annexed by the United States, and in 1959 it became the 50th state.*

ACCESS

To organize the information in the chapter, make a timeline like the one on page 9. Make the last date 1959. (What happened then?) Fill in the timeline with dates from the chapter. For the first date, estimate when Polynesians first settled the Hawaiian Islands, using the following sentence from the chapter: *Polynesian sailors discovered [the Hawaiian Islands] long before Magellan set sail, maybe a thousand years before.* (Remember Magellan? If not, you can find more about him in Book One, *The First Americans*, or via the internet.)

WORD BANK   buccaneer   haoles   taboos

Complete the sentences below with words from the word bank. One word is not used.

1. Native Hawaiians called outsiders _____.

2. A _____ was another name for a pirate.

WITH A PARENT OR PARTNER

Compare the map on page 162 with the map on page 156. With a parent or partner, discuss the following questions. Write your answers in your history journal.

1. Where are the Hawaiian Islands in relation to the United States on page 156?

2. What U.S. possession was closest to Hawaii in 1898?

3. Where was Captain Cook on the map on page 156 before he sailed to Hawaii?

4. Locate the island of Hawaii on the map on 156. Locate Oahu. Where is Honolulu?

CRITICAL THINKING SEQUENCE OF EVENTS

Put B if the event described below happened before American missionaries landed in 1820. Put A if the event described happened after American missionaries landed.

_____ 1. Liliuokalani worked secretly on a new constitution.

_____ 2. He named them the Sandwich Islands, after a British aristocrat, the Earl of Sandwich, who was helping to pay bills for the trip.

_____ 3. Merchants, and others who saw opportunities, began arriving.

_____ 4. The Polynesians settled the islands and, for about 900 years, kept in contact with their home islands.

_____ 5. The Hawaiian religion was centered on a system of *kapus*—taboos.

_____ 6. The Hawaiian monarchy was finished.

_____ 7. The Hawaiians turned to the Americans for advice on laws, on other matters of government, and even on dress and ways of life.

_____ 8. He was Kamehameha I, and using guns and persuasion, he united the islands.

WRITING

In your history journal, write a diary entry for March 30, 1820. You are part of the missionary group. But instead of being upset about the appearance of the Hawaiians, you are astonished by the beauty of the island. Write at least four sentences.

SUMMARY *An assassin's bullet thrust Teddy Roosevelt into the White House. His energetic leadership style won him reelection and the power to reshape national and foreign policy.*

ACCESS

To organize the information in this chapter, make a main idea map in your history journal like the one on page 8. In the center of the organizer put *President "Teddy" Roosevelt.* Fill in the smaller circles with facts about Roosevelt's term in office.

WORD BANK   conflagration   trustbusting   malaria

Complete the sentences below with words from the word bank. One word is not used.

1. A _____ is a large fire.

2. Roosevelt made _____, passing laws to control enormous corporations, an important part of his time in office.

CRITICAL THINKING   FACT OR OPINION

A fact is a statement that can be proven. An opinion judges things or people, but cannot be proved or disproved. Put F or O in front of the sentences below from the chapter.

_____ 1.   Roosevelt made a great president.

_____ 2.   Roosevelt set a record that day: he shook 8,150 hands.

_____ 3.   All six children roller-skated in the basement, slid down the banisters, and played hide and seek in the attic.

_____ 4.   But Theodore Roosevelt wasn't just fun and games.

_____ 5.   President Roosevelt was responsible for the building of the Panama Canal.

_____ 6.   Nearly 6,000 men died, mostly from disease.

_____ 7.   Without Theodore Roosevelt it would have been even more difficult.

_____ 8.   After he helped settle a war between Japan and Russia he was given the Nobel Peace Prize.

MAP

Study the maps and diagrams on page 168. In your history journal, answer the questions below.

1. What direction would you travel if your ship traveled from the Pacific Ocean to the Caribbean Sea?

2. How far would your ship have to be lowered to travel Galliard Cut to the Pacific Ocean?

3. What locks would you pass through first if your ship went from Colón to Panama City?

4. About how many miles would your ship travel to cross the canal? About how many miles would that save a ship traveling from San Francisco to New York?

CHAPTER 32

JANE ADDAMS, REFORMER

SUMMARY *Jane Addams tackled the problems of urban poverty by going into the slums of Chicago to establish a community living and learning center. Her activism resulted in child-labor protections, public playgrounds, a juvenile court system, and garbage inspection.*

ACCESS

To organize the information in this chapter, make a main idea map in your history journal like the one on page 8. In the center of the organizer put *Chicago*. Fill in smaller circles with facts about poverty, immigrants, and Jane Addams.

WORD BANK   polyglot   pauperism   philosophers

Complete the sentences below with words from the word bank. One word is not used.

1. The word _____ comes from two Greek words meaning "many tongues."

2. People who struggle to survive are people who Addams called on the edge of "_____."

WITH A PARENT OR PARTNER

Study the map of immigrant groups in Chicago on page 173. With a parent or partner, discuss the following questions. Write your answers in your history journal.

1. Which immigrant group, if any, is part of your family background?

2. Where do immigrant groups live in your community?

3. Where are immigrant groups most likely to gather for events and celebrations?

CRITICAL THINKING SEQUENCE OF EVENTS

The sentences below describe the events in life of Jane Addams. Put 1, 2, 3, and so on in front of the sentences to describe what happened in chronological order.

_____ She bought a redbrick house, with white columns on the porch, in Chicago, right in the middle of the slums.

_____ Addams learned that reformers had to get involved in politics.

_____ Then Jane got tuberculosis, a common disease on those days.

_____ In 1931, when she was 71, Jane Addams was awarded the Nobel Peace Prize—the first American woman to be so honored.

_____ Hull House was so successful that it grew until there was 13 buildings and a staff of 65.

_____ She chose to do something important with her life.

_____ She got herself appointed a city garbage inspector.

WORKING WITH PRIMARY SOURCES

Read the words of Lincoln Steffens below. Answer the questions that follow.

> First in violence, deepest in dirt . . . an overgrown gawk of a—village, the 'tough' among cities. . . . Chicago likes audacity and . . . no matter who you are . . . Chicago will give you a chance.

1. What feelings do you get when you read that Chicago is an "overgrown gawk of a—village"?

2. What does the word "audacity" mean in the passage above?

3. What does Steffens dislike about Chicago?

4. What does Steffens like about Chicago?

WRITING

Imagine that you are a news reporter in the late 1800s. Study the news headlines on page 171. Choose one headline and write what you think the news article might have said to explain the headline.

HENRY FORD

SUMMARY *Henry Ford promised to "democratize the automobile," which up until then was affordable only for wealth people. By mass-producing an inexpensive car, he put the world on wheels and inspired a consumer culture.*

ACCESS

To organize the information in this chapter, make an outline like the one on page 8. For the title, write *Henry Ford*. For main ideas, put *Model T*, *Mars Production*, and *Workers*. Put at least two details under each main idea.

WORD BANK   mass production   assembly line   conveyor belt   automation   architect

Complete the sentences below with words from the word bank. One word is not used.

1. A _____, which brought car parts to workers standing in an

_____, was the key part of the factory system known as

_____.

2. _____, or working like robots, was the ultimate goal of Ford's system.

CRITICAL THINKING   DRAWING CONCLUSIONS

Each of the sentences in *italics* below is taken from the chapter. Put a check mark in front of all of the conclusions that can be drawn from reading the lines.

1. *Now, to any reasonable person at the turn of the century, the idea of an inexpensive car seemed nonsense.*

_____ (a) Cars were owned only by wealthy people at the turn of the century.

_____ (b) Most people used horses and wagons for transportation at the turn of the century.

_____ (c) Cars had not been invented at the turn of the century.

2. *When he was a boy, Ford became an apprentice in a machine shop.*

_____ (a) Ford learned mechanical skills early in life.

_____ (b) Ford became wealthy as an apprentice.

_____ (c) Most mechanical work was done in shops when Ford was young.

3. *In Henry Ford's factory a wide, moving belt, called a "conveyor belt," brought the car parts to the worker.*

_____ (a) Ford's factory was different from the machine shop where he had been an apprentice.

_____ (b) Ford workers stood in one place for hours each day.

_____ (c) Ford worked on the conveyor belt himself.

WORKING WITH PRIMARY SOURCES

Read the words of Charles Sorenson below. Answer the questions that follow.

> Regardless of earlier uses of some of these principles [interchangeable parts, conveyor belts, etc.] . . . mass production and its intensification into automation stems directly from what we worked out at Ford.

1. How do you know that mass production was used before these words were written?

2. What does the word "principles" mean in the passage above?

3. What does the word "intensification" mean in the words above?

4. Why do you think workers might dislike "mass production"?

34

THE BIRDMEN

SUMMARY *When Wilbur and Orville Wright left the ground in their "heavier-than-air-machine," people began to think anything was possible.*

ACCESS

To organize the information in this chapter, make a main idea map in your history journal like the one on page 8. In the center of the organizer put *Wright Brothers*. Fill in smaller circles with facts about their accomplishments.

WORD BANK   glider   wind tunnel   biplane   sprockets

Complete the sentences below with words from the word bank. One word is not used.

1. A _____ is an aircraft with long wings but no engine that flies on wind currents.

2. A _____ had two wings.

3. The Wright Brothers used a _____ to test the flow of air over various wing designs.

CRITICAL THINKING MAIN IDEA AND SUPPORTING DETAILS

Each sentences in italics below states a main idea from the chapter. Put a check mark in the blanks in front of the ONE sentence that DOES NOT support or tell more about the main idea.

1. *Wilbur was the older and more serious of the boys.*

_____ (a) Orville had a mischievous side.

_____ (b) Kings and presidents invited them for visits.

_____ (c) It was their mother who taught them mathematics and how to make things.

2. *Three problems needed solving in order for people to fly.*

_____ (a) Scientists call them lift, propulsion, and control.

_____ (b) Bikes, back at the end of the 19th century, were high-tech items.

_____ (c) Those problems had baffled some of the greatest scientific minds of all time.

WORKING WITH PRIMARY SOURCES

Read the words of Orville Wright below. In your history journal, answer the questions that follow.

> When my brother and I built . . . the first . . . flying machine, we thought . . . we were introducing into the world an invention which would make further wars practically impossible . . . [because] governments would realize the impossibility of winning by surprise attacks.

1. What two terms does Wright use to describe an airplane above?

2. How would airplanes make surprise attacks an "impossibility"?

3. What did the brother fail to understand about the uses of airplanes in war?

4. Why do you think the Wright Brother were disappointed that their planes did not end war?

WRITING

Imagine that you are a reporter and have seen the first flight on December 17, 1903. You race to the telegraph office to send the news to your home office. Write your message in your history journal. Limit the information to 35 words, just as Orville Wright did in the telegram on page 184.

CHAPTER 35

WILLIAM HOWARD TAFT

SUMMARY *Teddy Roosevelt helped put William Howard Taft into the White House. But when they disagreed, Roosevelt challenged Taft by starting his own political party. The split among Republicans thrust a new breed of progressive into the presidency—scholarly, serious Woodrow Wilson.*

ACCESS

To organize the information in this chapter, make a main idea map in your history journal like the one on page 8. In the center circle put *William Howard Taft*. Fill in smaller boxes with facts about Taft's term in office and his relationship with Teddy Roosevelt.

WORD BANK

Bull Moose Party   union movement   wage slaves   status quo   dollar diplomacy

Complete the sentences below with words from the word bank. One word is not used.

1. People who worked for low hourly pay were called _____.

2. The _____ was an attempt by workers to organize into groups that would work together to demand fair pay, decent hours, and worker safety from business leaders.

3. Most business leaders, however, preferred the _____, that is, keeping things as they were.

4. The _____, was a third political party led by Teddy Roosevelt that challenged Taft in the 1912 election.

WORKING WITH PRIMARY SOURCES

Read the words of John Dos Passos below. In your history journal, answer the questions that follow.

> Perhaps things weren't so bully any more; TR lost his voice during the triangular campaign . . . a maniac shot him in the chest, his life was saved by . . . the . . . manuscript of the speech. . . . TR delivered the speech with the bullet still in him . . . but the spell was broken.

1. What does the word "bully" mean in the excerpt above?

2. Whose presidential campaign is Dos Passos describing?

3. Why does Dos Passos call it a "triangular campaign"?

4. Why do you think Dos Passos means when he writes "the spell was broken"?

WRITING

Imagine that you are a reporter at the speech in Milwaukee and you witness the shooting described by Dos Passos on page 188. Use the information there, and your own imagination, to write a news report with the headline: *TR Shot at Campaign Stop!*

36 A SCHOOLTEACHER PRESIDENT

SUMMARY *Like Theodore Roosevelt, Woodrow Wilson turned childhood handicaps into strengths. Wilson had clearly defined progressive goals. However, like those other progressives, his agenda for change ignored one of the most glaring injustices of the early1900s—racism.*

ACCESS

To organize the information in this chapter, make a timeline of events in Woodrow Wilson's life based on inferences you can make. He was born four years before the Civil War—what year is that? What year did he learn to read? Most students graduate from college at age 21—what year was that for Wilson? He went to law school, back to graduate school, and became a professor. He was elected as governor and senator. Estimate in what years those events occurred based on knowing that he was elected president in 1912. Look up Wilson in an encyclopedia to see if your dates are correct.

WORD BANK   dyslexia   de facto   imperialist

Complete the sentences below with words from the word bank. One word is not used.

1. Some people who have difficulty learning to read have _____, a condition in which they see letters in words reversed.

2. _____ is another ways of saying "in fact" or "actually."

CRITICAL THINKING   FACT OR OPINION

A fact is a statement that can be proven. An opinion judges things or people, but cannot be proved or disproved. Put F or O in front of the sentences below from the chapter.

_____ 1. When Thomas Woodrow Wilson was nine he was still having trouble learning his ABCs.

_____ 2. Sometimes problems can become strengths.

_____ 3. He was the son, grandson, and nephew of ministers.

_____ 4. Politics was no career for a shy man.

_____ 5. He ran for governor of New Jersey.

_____ 6. Woodrow Wilson had steel in his bones and brains in his head.

_____ 7. In 1912, he was elected president of the United States.

_____ 8. Sometimes he was too sure of himself, and he wasn't good at understanding the other side's view of a problem.

WORKING WITH PRIMARY SOURCES

Read the words of Woodrow Wilson below. In your history journal, answer the questions that follow.

> Liberty has never come from Government. Liberty has always come from the subjects of it. . . . The history of liberty is a history of limitations of governmental power, not the increase of it.

1. What does the word "subjects" mean in the statement above?

2. What is another word for "liberty"?

3. What does Wilson mean by the phrase "limitations of governmental power"?

4. Write a statement in your own words that has the same meaning as Wilson's words.

WRITING

Study the cartoon on page 191. Write a caption that criticizes that Republicans for allowing Wilson to win office. Then write caption thanking the Republicans for their split that allowed Wilson to win.

WAR

SUMMARY *On April 2, 1917, Woodrow Wilson delivered a war message filled with idealism. "The world must be made safe for democracy," he declared. Privately he wept, knowing that the realities of war would soon shatter the optimism of the progressive era.*

ACCESS

In your history journal, join all of the timelines that you have assembled for this book into one large timeline from 1867 until 1917. Divide the years into ten-year periods. The first date—1867—should be the year that John Muir set out on his 1,000-mile walk. The last date should be April 2, 1917: the day the United States entered World War I.

WORD BANK

Central Powers   Allies   conscription   neutral   armistice   moat

Complete the sentences below with words from the word bank. One word is not used.

1. The _____ in the First World War included Germany and Austria.

2. The _____ in the First World War included France and Great Britain.

3. For the first three years of the war, the United States was _____: it did not take sides.

4. When war was declared, _____, also called a draft, was created that required all men between 21 and 30 to join the Armed Forces.

5. An _____ or peace agreement could not be reached before the United States entered the fighting.

WORKING WITH PRIMARY SOURCES

Read the words of Woodrow Wilson below. Answer the questions that follow in your history journal.

> But the right is more precious than peace, and we shall fight for . . . democracy, for the right of those who submit to authority to have a voice in their own government . . . for a universal domination of right by . . . free peoples as shall bring peace . . . to all nations.

1. What does the word "right" mean in the statement above?

2. How does Wilson define "democracy"?

3. What does Wilson mean by the phrase "universal domination of right"?

4. Write a statement in your own words that has the same meaning as Wilson's words.

WRITING

Make a list in your history journal of the "extremes" that you have read about throughout this book. List ten "very good" things about the period covered. List ten "very bad" things about the period covered.

LIBRARY/ MEDIA CENTER RESEARCH LOG

NAME _____

DUE DATE _____

What I Need to **Find**

I need to use:
- [ ] primary
- [ ] secondary

sources.

Places I **Know** to Look

Brainstorm: Other Sources and Places to Look

WHAT I FOUND

Rate each source from 1 (low) to 4 (high) in the categories below

helpful   relevant

How I Found it

Title/Author/Location (call # or URL)

Book/Periodical	Website	Other	Primary Source	Secondary Source	Suggestion	Library Catalog	Browsing	Internet Search	Web link

NAME _____

LIBRARY/ MEDIA CENTER RESEARCH LOG

DUE DATE _____

What I Need to **Find**

Places I **Know** to Look

Brainstorm: Other Sources and Places to Look

I need to use:

☐ primary
☐ secondary

sources.

WHAT I FOUND

Title/Author/Location (call # or URL)

☐ Book/Periodical
☐ Website
☐ Other

☐ ☐ ☐ ☐ ☐ ☐
☐ ☐ ☐ ☐ ☐ ☐
☐ ☐ ☐ ☐ ☐ ☐

☐ Primary Source
☐ Secondary Source

☐ ☐ ☐ ☐ ☐ ☐
☐ ☐ ☐ ☐ ☐ ☐

How I Found it

☐ Suggestion
☐ Library Catalog
☐ Browsing
☐ Internet Search
☐ Web link

☐ ☐ ☐ ☐ ☐ ☐
☐ ☐ ☐ ☐ ☐ ☐
☐ ☐ ☐ ☐ ☐ ☐
☐ ☐ ☐ ☐ ☐ ☐
☐ ☐ ☐ ☐ ☐ ☐

Rate each source from 1 (low) to 4 (high) in the categories below

helpful

relevant

Brainstorm: Other Sources and Places to Look

Places I **Know** to Look

What I Need to **Find**

I need to use: ☐ primary

☐ secondary sources.

WHAT I FOUND

Title/Author/Location (call # or URL)

How I Found it

Suggestion ☐
Library Catalog ☐
Browsing ☐
Internet Search ☐
Web link ☐

Primary Source ☐
Secondary Source ☐

Book/Periodical ☐
Website ☐
Other ☐

Rate each source from 1 (low) to 4 (high) in the categories below

helpful

relevant

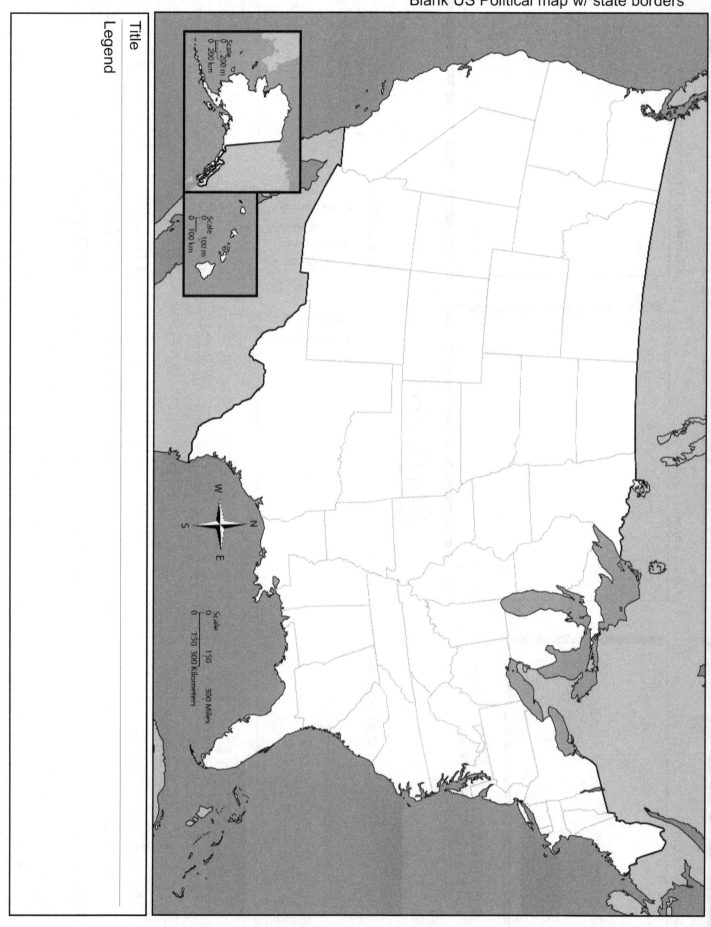

Title

Legend

Scale
0   200 m
0   200 km

Scale
0   100 m
0   100 km

W

S   N

E

Scale
0   150   300 Miles
0   150 300 Kilometers

Florida and the Carribean

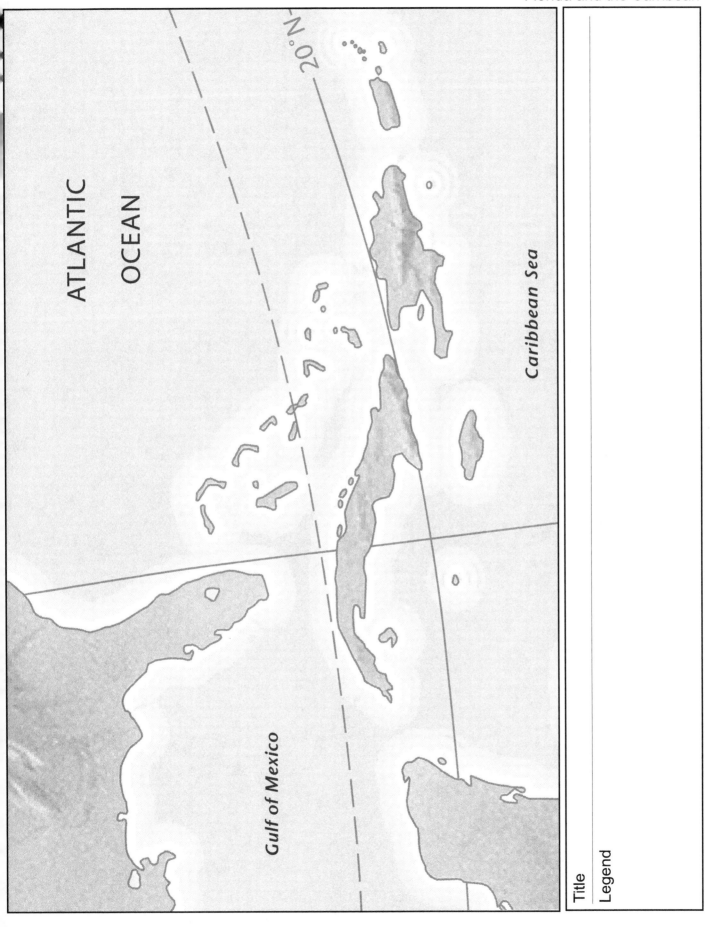

ATLANTIC OCEAN

Gulf of Mexico

Caribbean Sea

20° N.

Title

Legend

CPSIA information can be obtained
at www.ICGtesting.com
Printed in the USA
BVHW010045070320
574384BV00004B/72